# OREGON HISTORY

# SCORE KEY, TEST & TEST KEY

**ARPress**
ILLUMINATING IDEAS
EMPOWERING VOICES

**ARPress**
45 Dan Road Suite 5
Canton MA 02021

Hotline:          1(888) 821-0229
Fax:              1(508) 545-7580

Ordering Information:
Quantity sales. Special discounts are available on quantity purchases by corporations, associations, and others. For details, contact the publisher at the address above.

Printed in the United States of America.

ISBN-13:        Paperback        979-8-89389-121-8

Library of Congress Control Number: 2024909047

Effort has been made to locate sources and obtain permission for some of the graphic art and quotations used in this book. In the event of any unintentional omission, modifications will gladly be incorporated in future editions.

All Scripture quotations are from the
*New King James Version* except where noted.

# OREGON HISTORY

## SCORE KEY

**PAGE 1**

**Genesis 1:1**
In the beginning God created the heavens and the earth.
Vs. 9   Then God said, "Let the waters under the heavens be gathered together into one place, and let the dry land appear;" and it was so.
Vs. 10 And God called the dry land earth, and the gathering together of the waters He called seas. And God saw that it was good.

**John 1:1,2,3**   In the beginning was the Word, and the Word was with God, and the Word was God.
Vs. 2   He was in the beginning with God.
Vs. 3 all things were made through Him, and without Him nothing was made that was made.

**Genesis 7:19** And the waters prevailed exceedingly on the earth, and all the high hills under the whole heaven were covered.

**PAGE 2.**
1. extinct- 1) no longer living; having died out. 2) no longer burning or active.

2. elevation – 1) an elevating or being elevated. 2) a high place or position. 3) height above the surface of the earth.

3. geology – the study of the earth's crust and of the way in which it's layers were formed.

4. paleontology – the branch of geology that deals with prehistoric forms of life through the study of plant and animal fossils.

5. lava – 1) melted rock issuing from a volcano. 2) such rock when solidified by cooling.

6. fossil – 1) any rock or mineral dug out of the earth. 2) any hardened remains or traces of plant or animal life of some previous geological period, preserved in rock formations in the earth's crust.

7. secular humanist –
a. secular – of or relating to worldly things as distinguished from things relating to church.
b. 1) the quality of being human; human nature, a student of human nature and human affairs. 2) any system of thought or action based on the nature, dignity, interests, and ideals of man.

8. eon – an age, lifetime, eternity, an extremely long indefinite period of time.

9. atmosphere – 1) the gaseous envelope (air) surrounding the earth; consists of oxygen, nitrogen, and other gases, extends to a height of about 22,000 miles and rotates with the earth.

10. volcano – a vent in the earth's crust through which molten rock, (lava) rock fragments, gases, ashes, etc. are ejected from the earth's interior.

**Page 3**
1.   In the beginning God created the heavens and the earth.
2.   the study of the earth's crust and of the way in which it's layers were formed.
3.   a Big Bang
4.   lava
5.   water
6.   seashells
7.   Crater Lake
8.   Washington
9.   Cascade Range
10.   (any three) Mount Baker, Mount Rainier, Mount Hood, Mount Adams, Mount Jefferson, Mount Washington, and Mount Mazama

**Page 4**
1. a. Oregon     b. Asia
2. dog
3. a. language   b. customs   c. tribal
4. Native Americans
5. a. horse   b. buffalo

**Page 9**
1. Asia
2. white man

3. (two from this list)
    Alsea        Chinook        Clatsop  Coos
    Nehalem      Siletz         Siuslaw  Tillamook
    Salish       Yamhill

4. (two from this list)
    Calapooya        Cowlitz        Molalla
    Multnomah        Santiam

5. (four from this list)
    Cayuse    Columbia   Klamath   Modoc   Nez Perce
    Rogue     Snake      Umatilla  Umpqua  Wasco

6. (four from this list)
    Bannock          Nez Perce        Paiute
    Shoshone Snake              Umatilla

**Page 10**

7. Coastal – lodges of cedar planks.
   Plains – teepee of buffalo, deer or elk hides.

8. River – dugout canoe, horses, walking.
   Plains – horse, travois, walking.

9. A crude sledge of the Native American Indians con-
   sisting of a net, or platform dragged along the
   ground on the two poles that support it and serve
   as shafts for the horse or dog pulling it.

10. Costal – hats, capes, and shirts woven from plant

fiber. Skins of seal, otter and muskrat.
Plains – hides from buffalo, deer, bear and rabbit,
all made into shirts, dresses, pants and robes.

1. Woman in Rain
2. Little woman in wagon

**Page 18**
Circumnavigation: To sail or fly around the earth, an
island, etc.

**Page 19**
Test Your Memory

1.  C          11.  F
2.  E          12.  F
3.  B          13.  T
4.  F          14.  T
5.  J          15.  T
6.  A          16.  a. Captain Bruno Heceta
7.  H               b. Captain James Cook
8.  D               c. Captain John Meares
9.  G               d. Captain George Vancouver
10. I               e. Captain Robert Gray

17. In the beginning God created the heavens and the
    earth.
18. a. Coastal b.  River
    c.  Valley            d.  Plains or Horse

# UNIT II  *Exploration Westward and Mountain Men*

**Page 22**
1. Thomas Jefferson
2. Louisiana Purchase
3. Napoleon Bonaparte
4. a. Lewis    b. Clark
5. Corps of Discovery

**Page 23**
1. pirogues
2. Mandan
3. Sacaqawea
4. Shoshone
5. Minnetaree
6. rattlesnake rattle
7. Janey
8. Pompii
9. York
10. "wet finger rubbing" test

**Page 24**
1. grizzley
2. Scannon
3. Shining Mountains
4. horses
5. blanket

**Page 25**
1. Cameahwait
2. brother
3. a. Continental Divide
   b. west
4. topography – the accurate and detailed description of
   a place.

5. pirogues – a canoe made by hollowing out a large
   log. Any canoe shaped boat.

6. portage – the act of carrying or transporting overland
   between navigable rivers, lakes, etc.

7. pelt – the skin of a fur bearing animal, esp. after it has been stripped from the carcass.

8. rendezvous – a place designated for a meeting or assembly, as of troops, ships, airplanes.

9. bastion – 1) a projection from a fortification, arranged to give a wider firing range. 2) any forti-fied place; strong defense or bulwark.

10. evaporation – 1) to change (a liquid or solid) into vapor; drive out or draw off in the form of vapor. 2) to remove moisture from (milk, vegetables, fruits, etc.) by heating or drying so as to get a concentrat-ed product.

**Page 27**
1. November
2. Fort Clatsop
3. Christmas
4. March
5. 4,000

**Page 29**
1. hill
2. 60 pounds
3. muffoon
4. felt
5. ladies

**Page 30**
1. Jacob Astor
2. Tonquin
3. overland
4. an explosion of the powder magazine
5. Fort Astoria

**Page 32**
1. Fort Astoria
2. Fort George
3. castoreum
4. Jedediah Smith

**Page 33**
1. a. 1818   b. Oregon Country
2. Fort Vancouver

**Page 34**
3. factor
4. six
5. John Ball

1. Any Territory which either Great Britain or the United States acquired during the War of 1812, should be returned to it's former owner.
2. a. United States    b. Great Britain
3. a. Oregon          d. parts of British Columbia
   b. Washington      e. parts of Wyoming
   c. Idaho           f. Montana
4. Fort Vancouver
5. factor    John McLoughlin
6. John Ball
7. Headed Eagle
8. yes
9. Father of Oregon
10. a. Oregon City   b. resigned

**Page 35**

Test Your Memory

1. F
2. T
3. T
4. T
5. F
6. F
7. T
8. F
9. F
10. T

11. horses
12. Corps of Discovery
13. Continental Divide
14. Fort Clatsop
15. a. 1805   b. 1806
16. salt
17. beaver
18. muffoon
19. hats
20. John Jacob Astor
21. a. rendezvous
    b. beaver pelts
22. Bridger
23. Provided that any territory which either Great Britain or the United States, acquired during the War of 1812 should be returned to the former owner.
24. McLoughlin
25. Vancouver

**Page 38**
1. a. north-west    b. white men
2. Heaven
3. a. Indians    b. flattened    c. heads
4. a. Cowlitz    b. Chinook
5. no

**Page 39**
1. Reverend Jason Lee        Flathead
2. September
3. French Prairie
4. Cyrus Shepard

**Page 41**
1. a. Anna Maria Pittman    b. July 16, 1837
2. white woman
3. die
4. Lucy Anna Maria
5. a. life            b. corruption
   c. family          d. Good news

**Page 42**
1. Marcus Whitman
2. cholera
3. a. arrowhead    b. Jim Bridger
4. Narcissa Prentiss

**Page 43**
1. a. Independence Rock
   b. "register"
2. Continental Divide
3. Boise
4. Nez Perce
5. Cayuse

**Page 44**
1. Continental Divide
2. Alice Clarissa
3. White Fawn
4. Hawaiian
5. Nez Perce

**Page 45**
1. a. Catholic
   b. Blanchet
2. French Prairie
3. unspoiled tribes of the Interior
4. Flathead

**Page 46**
1. two years old
2. a. Daniel Webster
   b. Horace Greeley
3. forts
4. "saved"
5. missionary – a person sent on a mission, a person sent out by a church to preach, teach, and proselytize, as in a foreign country considered heathen.

6. commitment – 3) a pledge or promise to do something. 4) a financial liability undertaken, as an agreement to buy or sell securities.

7. cholera – jaundice, nausea, bile, yellow, green, any of several intestinal diseases.
   (Taken from Taber's Cyclopedic Medical Dictionary)
   An acute, specific infections disease characterized by diarrhea with severe loss of fluids and electrolytes; painful cramps of muscles; and tendency to collapse. Transmission is through water, milk, or other foods contaminated with excreta of patients or carriers. Incubation, a few hours to four to five days.
   Four stages: 1. Invasion   2. Evacuation
                3. Collapse   4. Stage of Reaction
   PREVENTION: Proper sanitation.

8. manufacture – the making of goods and articles by hand or esp., by machinery, often on a large scale and with division of labor.

9. accompany – 1) to go or be together with; attend. 2) to send; add to; supplement.

10. establish – 1) to make stable; make firm; settle. 2) to order, ordain, or enact (a law, statute, etc.) permanently. 3) to set up (a government, nation, business).

11. disgruntled – to make peevishly discontented; displease and make sulky.

12. respect – 1) to feel or show honor or esteem for; hold in high regard. 2) to consider or treat with deference or dutiful regard.

13. register – a record or list of names, items, etc., often kept by an official appointed to do so.

14. encourage – 1) to give courage, hope, or confidence to; embolden; hearten. 2) to give support to; be favorable to; foster; help.

**Page 48**
1. a. morals          b. manners
2. a. discipline       b. or hardwork
3. a. measles  b. smallpox
   c. dysentery        d. influenza
4. a. 1847             b. Cayuse
5. no resistance
6. Tomahas
7. 13
8. Circuit Rider Pastor
9. no
10. Golden Rule
11. a. ideals    b. fear God
    c. keep His Commandments
12. place to live

1. C
2. B
3. I
4. G
5. A
6. D
7. E
8. F
9. J
10. H
11. Jason Lee
12. Doctor Marcus Whitman
13. Father Francis Blanchet
14. Place of the Rye Grass
15. Cayuse
16. French Prairie
17. Hawaiian Islands
18. Horace Greeley
19. forts
20. Tomahas
21. 13
22. yes
23. Circuit Rider Pastor
24. Golden Rule
25. keep His Commandments

# UNIT IV    *The Oregon Trail, Wagon Trains & Wolf Meetings*

**Page 51**
**Romans 13:2**
Therefore whoever resists the authority resists the ordinance of God, and those who resist will bring judgment on themselves.
**Vs. 3** For rulers are not a terror to good works, but to evil. Do you want to be unafraid of the authority? Do what is good, and you will have praise from the same.

**Page 52**
1. Ewing Young
2. Jason Lee          laws
3. Wolf meetings
4. sheriff
5. Oregon City
6. optimism– 1) the doctrine held by Leibniz and others that the existing world is the best possible. 2) the doctrine or belief that good ultimately prevails over evil.

7. curiosity – 1) a desire to learn or know. 2) a desire to learn about things that do not properly concern one; inquisitiveness.

8. parallel – 1) extending in the same direction and at the same distance apart at every point, so as never to meet, as lines, planes, etc.

9. inherit – 1) to transfer property to (an heir). 2) to receive (property, a title, etc.) by the laws of inheritance from an ancestor at his death.

10. ransom – the redeeming or release of a captive or of seized property by payment of money or compliance with other demands.

11. epidemic – among the people, general prevalent and spreading rapidly among many individuals in a community at the same time; widespread: said esp. of a human contagious disease.

12. emigrants – 1) emigrating. 2) of emigrants of emi-
    gration, a person who emigrates. (one who moves
    away, to leave one country or region to settle in
    another.)

**Page 55**
1.  May 22, 1843
2.  a.  Pioneering instinct    b.  optimism
    c.  curiosity
3.  oxen
4.  $150
5.  one good rifle and a shotgun
6.  any from this list:
    Chimney Rock
    Scotts Bluff
    Fort Laramie
    Independence Rock
    South Pass
    Fort Boise
    Grande Ronde
    Columbia River
    The Dalles                Barlow Road
    Fort Vancouver            Oregon City
1.  five
2.  a.  grizzly bears    b.  rattlesnakes
    c.  cholera          d.  getting lost

**Page 57**
1.  a.  Jesse Applegate
    b.  A Day With the Cow Column
2.  12 to 15
3.  a.  Platte River    b.  bottom side up
4.  a.  rafts           b.  Columbia River
5.  Great Emigration

**Page 59**
1.  a.  James K. Polk
    b.  May
    c.  1845
2.  1,000
3.  1,400
4.  5,000
5.  a.  forts    b.  wagon trains

6.  **Isaiah 49:11-12**
    I will make each of my mountains a road, and my
    highways shall be elevated. Surely these shall come
    from afar; Look! Those from the north and the
    west, and these from the land of Sinim.

**Page 60**
1.  Never made a mountain but what He provided a
    place for man to go over or around it.
2.  Tygh Valley
3.  Rector
4.  Fort Deposit
5.  William Berry

**Page 61**
1.  a.  Sam Barlow    b.  1846
2.  Phillip Foster
3.  $5.00
4.  $2.50
5.  J.W.Ladd

**Fill in the blanks**
**Page 61**
1.  a.  Aberdeen    b.  49th
2.  a.  George Abernathy
    b.  J.Quinn Thornton
        3.  slavery

**Page 62**
1.  a.  small pox    b.  cholera    c.  measles
2.  100,000
3.  30,000
4.  Cayuse   Whitman    11
5.  Helen
6.  Medicine man

**Page 63**
1.  Eliza Spalding
2.  Joe Meek
3.  President James Polk
4.  a.  49th parallel - north
    b.  42nd parallel – south
    c.  Continental Divide - east
    d.  Pacific Ocean - west
5.  General Joseph Lane
6.  Marshall

**Page 64**
1.  13,000
2.  a.  320    b.  320
3.  a.  land    b.  gold
4.  Gold

**Page 66**
**Psalms 119:127**
    Therefore I love your commandments more than
    gold, yes, than fine gold!

**Matthew 5:13**

But if the salt loses it's flavor, how shall it be seasoned? It is then good for nothing but to be thrown out and trampled underfoot by men.

1. Jacksonville
2. a. tough    b. supplies

**Page 67**
3. 1853
4. a. salt    b. gold
5. greased

**Fill in the blanks**
**Page 67**
1. $13,000,000
2. a. copperb. tin    c. cinnabar
   d. gold          e. silver
3. panning
4. rocker

**Page 68**
1. water
2. Dredges

**Page 69**
3. tailings
4. a. dust    b. flakes    c. nuggets
5. Blue Bucket Mine
6. oranges

**Isaiah 45:12**

I have made the earth, and created man on it. It was I – my hands that stretched-out the heavens, and all their host I have commanded.

1. Chinese
2. 25 cents
3. Chinatown
4. Joss Houses

**Test Your Memory**
**Page 70**
1. B
2. C
3. C
4. A
5. C
6. C
7. B
8. C
9. B
10. C

11. Polk
12. forts
13. Sam Barlow
14. a. cholera    b. measles
15. Joseph Lane
16. marshal
17. 320
18. gold
19. a. placer    b. hardrock
20. a. flakes    b. dust    c. nuggets
21. Blue Bucket Mine

# UNIT V  *Government and Statehood*

**Page 74**
1. a. 1859    b. James Buchanan
   c. 33rd
2. Salem
3. Stumptown
4. Lovejoy
5. Lot Whitcomb
6. a. Ainsworth
   b. Oregon Steam Navigation Company
7. $10,000

**Page 75**
1. a. Rogue River War    b. Modoc War
   c. Nez Perce War
2. Rogue River Indians
3. a. 1856    b. Gold Beach
4. Captain Jack
5. Mary

6. Queen of the Modocs
7. General Canby

**Page 76**
1. Shahaptain
2. a. Joseph    b. Henry Spalding
3. Hin May Too Yah Lat Kekht
4. Thunder Rolling in the Mountains
5. "Don't ever sell the bones of your ancestors."

**Page 77**
1. a. U.S.Grant    b. O.O.Howard
   c. Wallowa
2. a. Joesph    b. peace
3. 30
4. Junction of White Bird Creek and Salmon River, White Bird Canyon
5. Nez Perce

**Page 79**
1.  Grandmother's land
2.  a. Sitting Bull    b.  Sioux
3.  1,300
4.  a.  5    b. Bird Canyon
5.  September 30, 1877
6.  Ollikut
7.  1877
8.  Miles
9.  "From where the sun now stands, I will fight no
    more, forever."

**Page 80**
1.  Ben Holladay
2.  a.  east siders        b.  railroad
3.  a.  Portland          b.  Eugene
4.  a.  1872             b.  Roseburg

**Page 81**
1.  California
2.  Ashland
3.  200    700
4.  7 days
5.  38 hours

**Define the following:**

1. interpreter – a person who interprets; specif., a person whose work is translating a foreign language
   orally, as in a conversation between people speaking
   different languages.

2. treaty – 1) negotiation. 1b.) entreaty  1c.) any agreement or contract 2a.) a formal agreement between
   two or more nations, relating to peace, alliance,
   trade, etc

3.  retreat – 1) a going back or backward; withdrawal
    in the face of opposition or
    from a dangerous or unpleasant situation.

4.  escape – 1) to get free; get away; get out; break
    loose, as from a prison. 2) to avoid an illness; acci-
    dent, pain, etc.

5.  Indian reservation – Public land set aside for some
    special use (an Indian reservation, military reserva-
    tion.)

6.  stockade – 1) a barrier of stakes driven into the
    ground side by side, for defense against attach.
    2) an enclosure, as a fort, made with such stakes.

7.  tactic – 2) a detail or branch of tactics – tactical of
    or having to do with tactics,  esp. in military or
    naval maneuvers.

8.  bankrupt – 1) a person legally declared unable to
    pay his debts: the property of a bankrupt is admin-
    istered for the benefit of his creditors and divided
    among them.

9.  elected – 1) chosen; given preference 2) elected but
    not yet installed in office (the mayor/elect.)

**Page 83**
1.  a.  1890    b.  Spokane, Portland, Seattle Railroad
    Company
2.  a.  engineers    b.  fisherman
3.  east
4.  west

**Page 83**
**Proverbs 29:23**
    a man's pride will bring him low, but the humble in
    spirit will retain honor.
**Proverbs 16:18**
    Pride goes before destruction, and a haughty spirit
    before a fall.

**Page 84**
1.  rocks
2.  a. murder
    b. assault
3.  hazard of the railroad building business.
4.  Chinese
5.  20 to 30 cents
6.  pride
7.  a.  cease-fire    b.  1910
8.  golden    Bend
9.  218
Suffrage
    2) a vote or voting;
    esp., a vote in favor
    of some candidate
    or issue. 3) the right
    to vote, esp. in
    political elections;
    franchise.

**Page 85**
1. men
2. Suffrage –
   2) a vote or voting; esp., a vote in favor of some candidate or issue. 3) the right to vote, esp. in political elections; franchise.
3. a. Scott   b. 1852
4. Benjamin C. Duniway
5. newspaper
6. The New Northwest
7. The Oregonian
8. a. 1   b. 5
9. a. 1912   b. vote

**Page 86**
1. 1846
2. Fort Hall
3. a. Salem   b. Christmas
4. a. coin   b. picayune
5. six cents
6. school
7. a. reading   b. writing   c. arithmetic
8. Pacific University

**Page 88**
1. Feb. 14, 1859
2. a. Legislative   b. Executive   c. Judicial
3. a. Senate   b. House of Representatives
4. a. 21   b. citizen   c. three
5. a. four   b. two

Veto – 1) an order prohibiting some proposed or intended act; prohibition, esp. by a person in authority. 1b) the power to prevent action by such prohibition.
1. a. 30   b. citizen   c. three
2. commander in chief
3. veto
4. a. Governor
   b. Secretary of State
   c. State Treasurer
   d. Labor Commissioner
   e. Attorney General

**Page 89**
1. a. State Supreme Court
   b. Court of Appeals
   c. lesser courts
2. punishment
3. William S. U'Ren
4. Switzerland
5. a. starting
   b. stopping
6. mayor
7. manager
8. government
9. a. Warm Springs Indians
   b. Umatilla Indians
   c. Klamath Indians

**Page 90**
1. Oswald West
2. a. 400   b. public use
3. vote
4. 1912
5. Abigail Scott Duniway

**Famous People in Oregon**

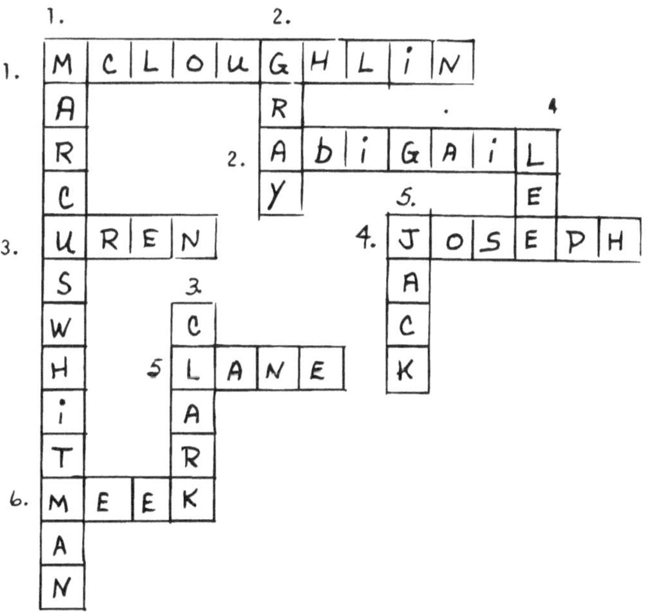


9

**Page 92**
1. a. 1859    b. Buchanan
2. Salem
3. Stumptown
4. Lot Whitcomb
5. John Ainsworth
6. a. Rogue River War
   b. Modoc War
   c. Nez Perce War
7. Captain Jack
8. Thunder Rolling in the Mountains

9. "Don't ever sell the bones of your ancestors."
10. Howard
11. 30
12. White Bird Creek
13. Grandmother's land
14. Nelson Miles
15. "from where the sun now stands, I will fight no
    more, forever."
16. a. James Hill    b. Edward Harriman
17. Abigail Scott Duniway
18. Tabitha Brown
19. a. Legislative    b. Executive    c. Judicial

# Unit VI    *Land and Animals*

**Page 96**
1. a. August    b. 1933
2. friction
3. a. Portland    b. 50
4. high velocity
5. a. sixty    b. seventy
6. a. crowned    b. leaped    c. jumped
7. fog
8. 311,000
9. Tillamook Burn

**Page 97**
1. a. man
   b. carelessness
2. a. west
   b. east
3. David Douglas
4. a. Goodyear Aerospace
   b. Triangular
5. a. ox
   b. railroads
   c. trucks

**Page 98**
1. construction
2. cellulose fiber
3. a. western hemlock
   b. Douglas fir
   c. lodgepole pine
   d. silver fir
4. a. mechanical
   b. chemical
5. a. Douglas fir
   b. peeler

Five products from this list.
flooring        siding for houses      wall paneling
furniture    counters    cabinets for the whole house

Define:
1. friction – 1) a rubbing, esp. of one object against
   another. 3) the resistance to motion of two moving
   objects or surfaces that touch.

2. botanist – a student of or specialist in botany. Botany
   – the science, a branch of biology, that deals with
   plants, their life, structure, growth, classification.

3. helium – one of the chemical elements, a very light,
   inert, colorless gas, having the lowest known boiling
   and melting points: it is used in low-temperature
   work, as a diluent for oxygen, for inflating balloons.

4. pungent – 1) producing a sharp sensation of taste
   and smell; acrid. 2) sharp and piercing to the mind;
   poignant; painful.

5. velocity – quickness or rapidity of motion or action;
   swiftness; speed.

**Page 100**
1. a. needleleaf        b. broadleaf
2. cone
3. a. 1939        b. Douglas fir
4. "Doug" fir
5. 200 feet
6. east
7. golden
8. sixty

1. flat
2. a. skirts        b. capes or hats
3. 200
4. 180 feet
5. stiff

6. aircraft
7. a. piano    b. organ    c. violin

**Page 101**
1. pungent
2. The juniper is like a camel because, it can live with less water than any other Oregon tree.
3. water
4. birch
5. red

**Page 102**
1. west
2. mistletoe
3. Acorns
4. six to twelve
5. western

**Page 103**
1. Laurel
2. camphor
3. Myrtle wood
4. a. Finished    b. hardwoods
5. answer to "Look for the word" – **SCANTLING**

Meaning: a small piece of lumber, a beam or timber.

**Page 107**
1. Cressman        sandals
2. Fort Rock
3. Radio-carbon or carbon 14
4. 9,000
5. a. baskets    b. knives or arrowheads    stones to weight nets
6. John Day Fossil Beds
7. Thomas Condon
8. a. plant    b. animal

Define:
navigation – 1) the act or practice of navigation; esp., the science of locating the position and plotting the course of ships and aircraft.

buoy – 1) a floating object anchored in a lake, river, etc. To warn of rocks, shoals, etc., or to mark a channel, and often equipped with a bell or light.

dredge – 2) an apparatus for scooping or sucking up mud, sand, rocks, etc., as in deepening or clearing channels, harbors, etc.

export – to carry or send (good, etc.,) to another country or other countries, esp., for purpose of sale.

grazing – 1) to feed on (growing grass, herbage, a pasture, etc.,) 2) to put livestock to graze on (growing grass, herbage, etc.)

**Page 109**
1. a. Columbia    b. deep water shipping lane to the ocean.
2. 110 miles
3. a. fresh    b. salt
4. 150
5. a. lighthouses    b. buoys
6. a. chain    b. bucket
7. 35 foot

**Page 110**
1. wood
2. a. iron    b. steel
3. naval mothball fleet
4. a. Newport    b. Coos Bay
5. lumber
6. wheat
7. a. Japan    b. China    c. Brazil
8. dry-dock
9. a. three    b. Swan Island    c. third

**Page 111**
1. specialty
2. Rye grass
3. a. lily    b. Curry
4. a. canning    b. freezing
5. wheat
6. three from this list:
   oats—barley—corn—alfalfa—timothy—clover

**Page 112**
1. a. beef        b. dairy
2. a. Hereford        b. Polled Hereford
   or  Aberdeen Angus
   or Shorthorns
3. a. equipment        b. grazing
4. population
5. a. Jersey
   b. Holstein
   c. Guernsey

**Page 113**
1. second
2. a. meat
   b. wool
3. egg
4. freezing

Food we grow in Oregon

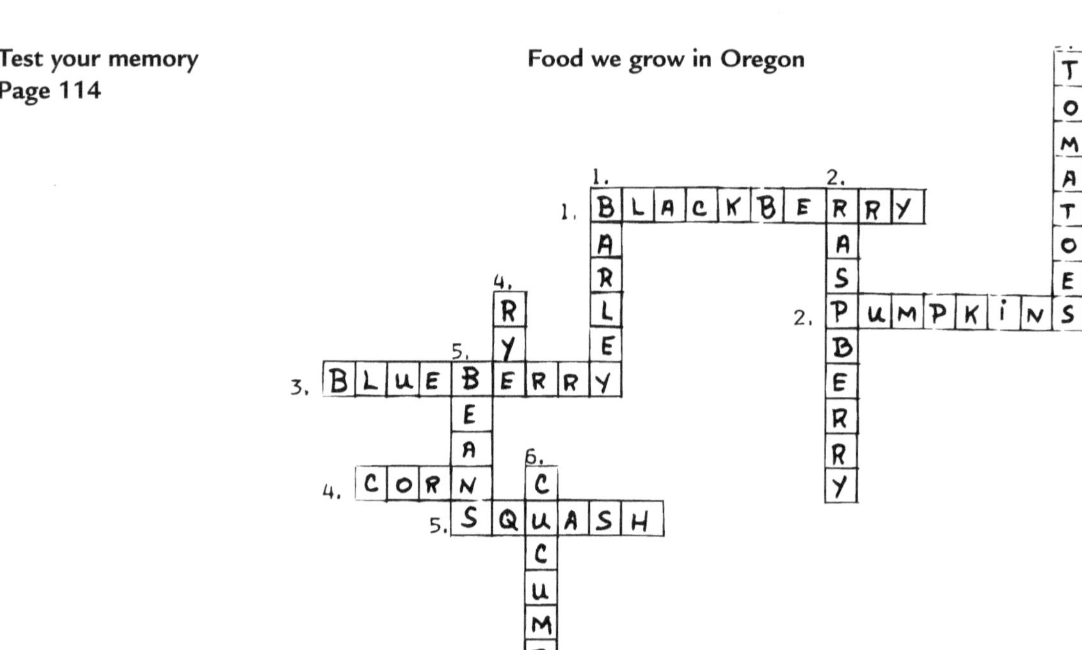


Multiple choice:  Matching:

| | | | |
|---|---|---|---|
| 1. C | 10. H | 19. L | |
| 2. B | 11. K | 20. F | |
| 3. C | 12. D | | |
| 4. B | 13. M | | |
| 5. B | 14. A | | |
| 6. C | 15. N | | |
| 7. E | 16. G | | |
| 8. I | 17. J | | |
| 9. B | 18. C | | |

True or False
21. F
22. F
23. T
24. T
25. T

# Unit VII  Oregon Facts

**Page 123**

Define:

1. escutcheon – a shield or shield-shaped surface on which a coat of arms is displayed.

2. diameter – a straight line passing through the center of a circle, sphere, etc. from one side to the other side.

3. omnivorous – eating any sort of food; esp. both animal and vegetable food.

4. geode – a globular stone having a cavity lined with inward growing crystals or layers of silica.

5. transparent – transmitting light rays so that objects on the other side may be distinctly seen; capable of being seen through; neither opaque nor translucent.

**Page 124**

| | | |
|---|---|---|
| 1. I | | 14. W |
| 2. P | | 15. G |
| 3. E | | 16. O |
| 4. R | | 17. N |
| 5. K | 18. H | |
| 6. C | | 19. Y |
| 7. U | | 20. B |
| 8. M | | 21. S |
| 9. F | | 22. L |
| 10. T | | 23. D |
| 11. A | 24. V | |
| 12. Q | 25. X | |
| 13. J | | |

**Page 146**

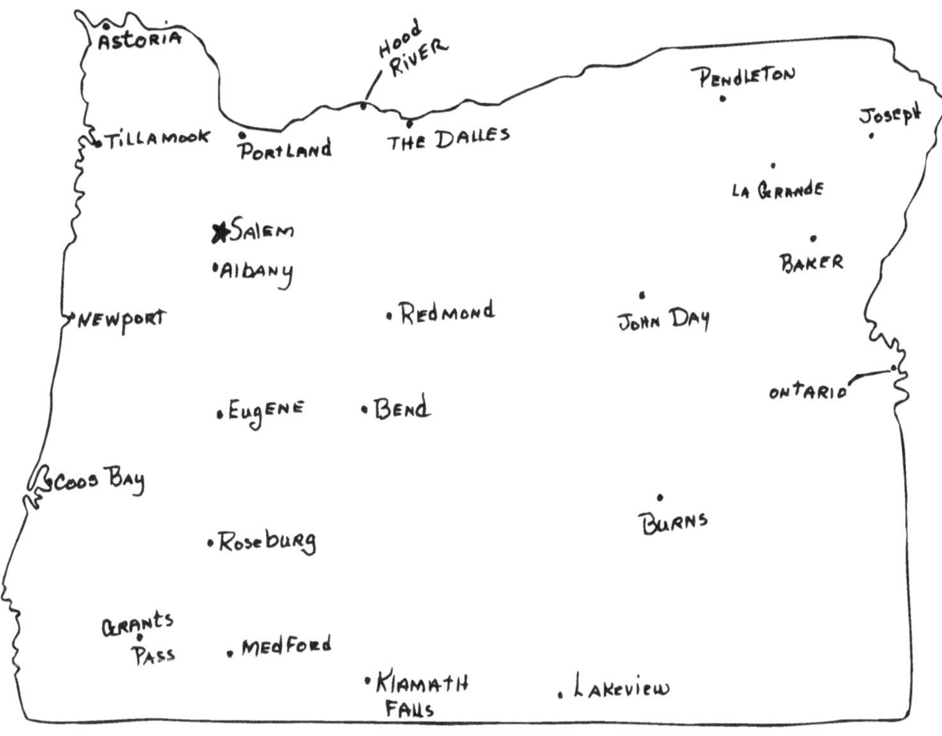


**Page 147**

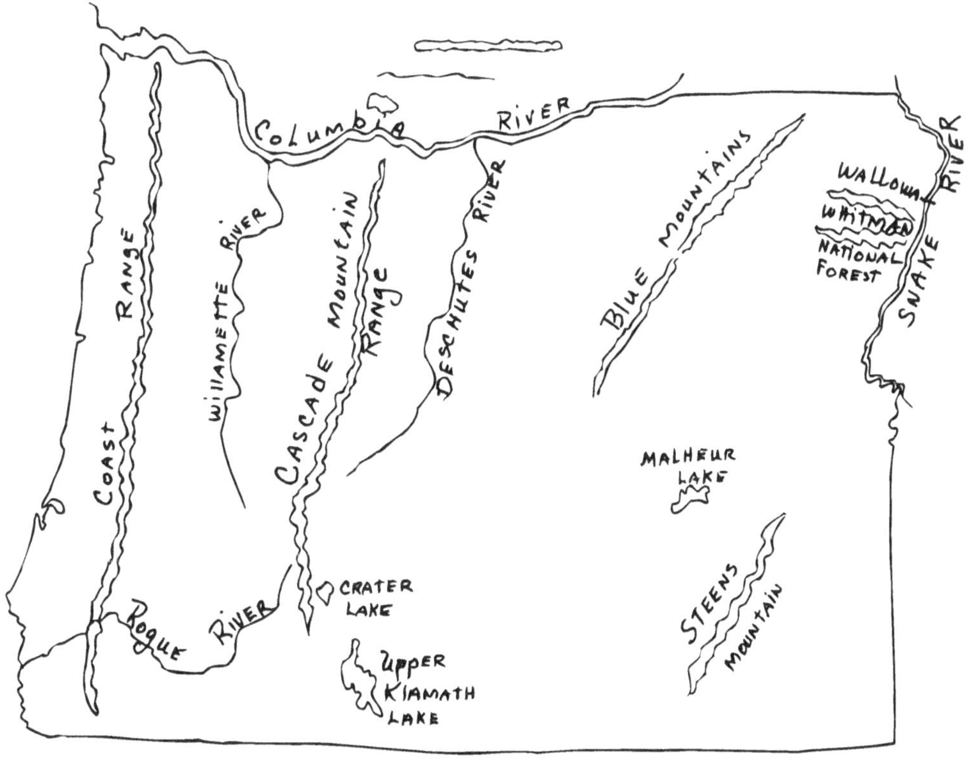

**Cities of Oregon**

# OREGON
# HISTORY

## TEST

| **Unit I** | **FINAL TEST ANSWERS:**  (4 points each) |
| --- | --- |

| | |
| --- | --- |
| 1.  F | 11. radio carbon test / carbon 14 |
| 2.  T | 12. Robert Gray |
| 3.  F | 13. Big Bang |
| 4.  T | 14. a. Coastal   b. River   c. Valley   d. Plains |
| 5.  F | 15. Washington |
| 6.  F | 16. George Vancouver |
| 7.  F | 17. "In the beginning God created the heavens and the earth." |
| 8.  T | 18. a. Captain Bruno Hecete      d. Captain Robert Gray |
| 9.  T |     b. Captain James Cook      e. Captain George  Vancouver |
| 10.  F |     c. Captain John Meares |

## Unit II    FINAL TEST ANSWERS     (4 points each)

| | | |
| --- | --- | --- |
| 1.  F | 11. salt | 21. Corps of Discovery |
| 2.  F | 12. horses | 22. rendezvous |
| 3.  T | 13. John Jacob Astor | 23. Fort Clatsop |
| 4.  F | 14. beaver | 24. 1805—1806 |
| 5.  F | 15. Bridger | 25. Any territory which either Great |
| 6.  T | 16. McLoughlin |     Britain or the United States |
| 7.  T | 17. Continental Divide |     acquired during the War of 1812 |
| 8.  T | 18. muffoon |     should be returned to it's |
| 9.  F | 19. Vancouver |     former owner. |
| 10.  F | 20. hats | |

## Unit III    FINAL TEST ANSWERS (4 points each)

| | | |
| --- | --- | --- |
| 1.  b | 10.  b | 19.  T |
| 2.  c | 11.  T | 20.  T |
| 3.  c | 12.  T | 21.  F |
| 4.  c | 13.  F | 22.  T |
| 5.  c | 14.  T | 23.  F |
| 6.  b | 15.  T | 24.  T |
| 7.  c | 16.  F | 25.  F |
| 8.  c | 17.  F | |
| 9.  b | 18.  F | |

## UNIT IV    FINAL TEST ANSWERS        (4points each)

| | | |
| --- | --- | --- |
| 1.  F | 10.  T | 19.  c |
| 2.  F | 11.  b | 20.  c |
| 3.  F | 12.  a | 21.  b |
| 4.  T | 13.  b | 22.  b |
| 5.  T | 14.  b | 23.  c |
| 6.  F | 15.  c | 24.  b |
| 7.  F | 16  b | 25.  a |
| 8.  T | 17.  c | |
| 9.  F | 18.  a | |

## UNIT V    FINAL TEST ANSWERS(5 points each)

| | | |
| --- | --- | --- |
| 1.  b | 8.  a | 15.  A |
| 2.  c | 9.  c | 16.  D |
| 3.  b | 10.  b | 17.  J |
| 4.  c | 11.  I | 18.  G |
| 5.  a | 12.  C | 19.  F |
| 6.  b | 13.  E | 20.  B |
| 7.  b | 14.  H | |

## UNIT VI     FINAL TEST ANSWER          (4 Points each)

1.   a. Tillamook Burn          11. G          21. A
     b. Portland               12. C          22. B
2.   friction                  13. J          23. C
3.   sandals                   14. E          24. ALL THREE
4.   cone                      15. A
5.   110                       16. H
6.   Swan Island               17. D
7.   Jersery/Guernsey/Holstein 18. I
8.   aircraft or airplane      19. F
9.   camphor                   20. B
10.  vee-balloons

## UNIT VII       FINAL TEST ANSWERS          (4 points each)

1. Salem                       11. D          21. a
2. Feb. 14, 1859               12. I          22. b
3. Navy Blue and Gold          13. F          23. c
4. milk                        14. C          24. b
5. Chinook Salmon              15. G          25. b
6. Oregon Grape                16. A
7. Western Meadowlark          17. J
8. Oregon Sunstone             18. E
9. Thunder egg                 19. H
10. "Oregon My Oregon"         20. B

## UNIT VIII     FINAL TEST ANSWERS          (2 points each)

### COUNTIES

| | | | | | |
|---|---|---|---|---|---|
| BAKER | CROOK | HARNEY | LAKE | MORROW | UNION |
| BENTON | CURRY | HOOD RIVER | LANE | MULTNOMAH | WALLOWA |
| CLACKAMAS | DESCHUTES | JACKSON | LINCOLN | POLK | WASCO |
| CLATSOP | DOUGLAS | JEFFERSON | LINN | SHERMAN | WASHINGTON |
| COLUMBIA | GILLIAM | JOSEPHINE | MALHEUR | TILLAMOOK | WHEELER |
| COOS | GRANT | KLAMATH | MARION | UMATILLA | YAMHILL |

### COUNTY SEATS

| | | |
|---|---|---|
| BAKER CITY | BURNS | HEPPNER |
| CORVALLIS | HOOD RIVER | PORTLAND |
| OREGON CITY | MEDFORD | DALLAS |
| ASTORIA | MADRAS | MORO |
| ST. HELENS | GRANTS PASS | TILLAMOOK |
| COQUILLE | KLAMATH FALLS | PENDLETON |
| PRINEVILLE | LAKEVIEW | LA GRANDE |
| GOLD BEACH | EUGENE | ENTERPRISE |
| BEND | NEWPORT | THE DALLES |
| ROSEBERG | ALBANY | HILLSBORO |
| CONDON | VALE | FOSSIL |
| CANYON CITY | SALEM | McMINNVILLE |

**THE TEACHER WILL NEED TO GRADE THE REPORTS WRITTEN BY THE STUDENTS FOR THE NEXT 150-WORD REPORTS AND THE 250-WORD REPORTS.**

# OREGON HISTORY

# TEST KEY

# OREGON HISTORY STUDENT WORKBOOK

## FINAL TESTS

THESE ARE THE FINAL TESTS FOR THE EIGHT UNITS OF THE OREGON HISTORY STUDENT WORKBOOK.

> **YOU HAVE THE PERMISSION OF THE AUTHOR AND THE PUBLISHER TO RE-PRODUCE AS MANY COPIES OF THE FINAL TESTS, AND THE FINAL TESTS ONLY, AS NEEDED.**

## UNIT 1     FINAL TEST 4 points each

## TRUE OR FALSE

1. _______ Mount St. Helens erupted in the state of Idaho.
2. _______ The Cascade Range runs north and south.
3. _______ Captain George Vancouver found the Columbia River.
4. _______ The first people to come to the Oregon Country were from Asia.
5. _______ The buffalo made it easy for the Indians to travel.
6. _______ The hot liquid coming from a volcano is called granite.
7. _______ Bones of buffalo were found at high elevations.
8. _______ Capt. John Meares built a trading post at Nootka Sound.
9. _______ Crater Lake is found in the crater of what used to be called Mount Mazama.
10. _______ Captain Bruno Heceta blew up the ship Columbia.

**Fill in the blank**

11. The special test used to tell us the age of plants and animals is called?
    __________________________________.
12. Captain _______________________________ found and named the Columbia River.
13. Some secular humanist scientist say the earth started with a? _______________
    _______________.
14. Name the four Indian groups in Oregon.
    a. _________________________________,
    b. _________________________________,
    c. _________________________________,
    d. _________________________________.
15. In what state is Mount St. Helens? _________________________________________
16. Mount Baker was named by Captain ______________ _________________.
17. What does Genesis 1:1 tell us? ___________________________________________
    __________________________________________________.
18. List the names of five ships' captains who explored the Pacific Northwest
    Coastline since Sir Francis Drake in 1587.
    a. _________________________________________
    b. _________________________________________
    c. _________________________________________
    d. _________________________________________
    e. _________________________________________

## Unit II        Final Test     4 points each

### True or False

1. _______Susie was the nickname of Sacagawea.
2. _______Chief Joseph was the brother of Chief Cameahwait.
3. _______The expedition needed horses to cross the mountains.
4. _______The Blackfoot Indians kidnapped Sacagawea.
5. _______Napoleon Bonaparte was the President of the United States in 1803.
6. _______Lewis and Clark were picked by Thomas Jefferson.
7. _______The western mountains were called The Shining Mountains by the Indians.
8. _______The Louisiana Purchase was bought from France.
9. _______Billy was the nickname of Sacagaweas' son.
10. _______Spot was the name of  Lewis' dog.

### Fill in the Blank

11. Ocean water was boiled to get? ________________
12. The expedition got __________________from the Shoshone Indians.
13. The first official trading post was built at Astoria and named after?

    ______________  __________  ______________.
14. The __________________ was trapped for its fur.
15. Two famous mountain men were, Jedediah Smith and Jim __________________.
16. The chief factor was Dr. John ______________________________.
17. When all the water started to flow westward, the had crossed the?

    ____________________  ________________.
18. What was the name of the beaver's thick underfur? ________________
19. Dr. John was the man in charge of Fort ____________________.
20. Men and women wanted their _______________ made from this underfur.
21. What was the shortened name of Lewis and Clark expedition?

    ____________________  ______  ____________________.
22. It was at the ______________________________ that the mountain men met once a year.
23. Lewis and Clark built _________  __________________ at the southern part of the mouth of the Columbia River.
24. The expedition spent the winter of ________________and _______________ at the Pacific coast.
25. Explain the "Treaty of Ghent"

    ____________________________________________________________________________________

    ____________________________________________________________________________________

    ___________________________________________________________________________________.

24

## Unit III        Final Test      4 points each

## Multiple Choice

1. What was the name of the rock that was signed by the wagon train families?
   a. Pikes Peak            b. Independence Rock      c. Council Bluff

2.  Jason Lee married?
   a. Sacagawea            b. Narcissa Prentiss        c. Anna Maria Pittman

3. Dr. and Mrs. Whitman ministered to what Indians?
   a.  Clatsop Indians      b. Shoshone Indians        c.Cayuse

4. Who was the Indian that struck Dr. Whitman from behind?
   a. Captain Jack          b. Cameahwait              c. Tomahas

5. What was the name of Dr. Marcus Whitman's bride?
   a. Anna Maria Pittmanb. Abigail Scott   c. Narcissa Prentiss

6. The Whitman's settled at?
   a. Fort Vancouver        b. Waiilatpu              c. Fort Clatsop

7.  Marcus Whitman was a?
   a. Catholic              b. Methodist              c. Presbyterian preacher.

8.  Jason Lee settled at?
   a. French Prairie        b. Fort Clatsop          c. Mission Bottom

9. In New York City, Marcus Whitman saw?
   a. Thomas Jefferson    b. Horace Greeley        c. George Washington

10. Who sent the printing press?
   a.  Ladies Society        b.Hawaiian Mission       c. Hudson's Bay Company

## True or False

11. _______It was the white man's Book of Heaven that the Indians wanted to see.
12. _______ Joe Meek's daughter was killed at the Whitman's massacre.
13. _______ Jason Lee was a Presbyterian minister.
14. _______The Cowlitz and Chinook Indians were the tribes who flattened heads of the children.
15. _______The Circuit Rider Pastor followed the Golden Rule.
16. _______Jason Lee was a medical doctor.
17. _______Father Blanchet was a Methodist Missionary.
18. _______The printing press was kept at Fort Vancouver.
19. _______Dr. Whitman wanted more forts to be built along the trail.
20. _______Tomahas was the Indian who struck Dr. Whitman from behind.
21. _______Narcissa Whitman came by boat to the Northwest.
22. _______Marcus Whitman settled at Waiilatpu.
23. _______ At the Whitman massacre there were 22 people  killed.
24. _______The Circuit Rider Pastor admonished the people to fear
          God and to keep His Commandments.
25. _______ Jason Lee settled in Astoria.

## Unit IV        Final Test        4 points each

### TRUE OR FALSE:

1. _____ Joe Meek was the first territorial governor.
2. _____ The Donation Land grant gave a man 500 acres of land.
3. _____ The Columbia River was said to be so muddy, it flowed bottom up.
4. _____ Oxen were used to pull the wagons on the wagon train.
5. _____ Hardrock was one type of mining for gold.
6. _____ The basic cost for a family to come west was $5,000.
7. _____ Ewing Young was the first territorial sheriff.
8. _____ President James Polk was the president in 1845.
9. _____ The first capitol was at French Prairie.
10._____ Jesse Applegate wrote, A Day with the Cow Column.

### Multiple Choice:

11. The first sheriff of the Oregon territory was?
    a. Joseph Lane            b. Joe Meek            c. Ewing Young

12. There were three reasons families came to Oregon, one was pioneering  instinct, optimism and,    a. a. curiosi-
    ty                b. foolishness        c. boldness

13. The secret meetings were called?
    a. Fort member meetings        b. wolf meetings  c. Secret Society Meetings

14. Most of the wagon trains left Missouri around what month?
    a. September            b. May            c. February

15. The death of one man changed the course of history for Oregon.
    a. Jim Bridger            b. Joe Meek            c. Ewing Young

16. For years men have looked for what gold mine?
    a. Black Bart's Mine        b. Blue Bucket Mine        c. Pendleton Mine

17. The Indians defended their land from men who were seeking what?
    a. iron ore            b. uranium            c. gold

18. Joe Meek had been the sheriff but now he was the territorial?
    a. Marshall            b. Mayor            c. Governor

19. The first capitol was located at?
    a. Eugene            b. Portland            c. Oregon City

20. What was one of the diseases, the white man brought west?
    a.  scarlet fever        b. ringworm            c. measles

21. The president wanted more of what to be built along the trail?
    a. motels            b. forts            c. rendezvous

22. What did Sam Barlow build around the mountain?
    a. highway            b. road            c. fence line

23. Three types of gold were, dust, flakes and?
    a. boulders            b. sacks            c. nuggets

24. The first territorial governor was?
    a. Marcus Whitman        b. Joseph Lane        c. George Abernathy

25. What was the favorite animal to pull a wagon?
    a. oxen            b. horses            c. cows

## Unit V Final Test     5 points each

### Circle the answer:

1. The Nez Perce Indians headed for Canada and what they called?
   a. Father's land       b. Grandmother's land     c. Safety land

2. The name of the most famous Modoc Indian was?
   a.  Chief Joseph        b. Sitting Bull              c. Captain Jack

3. Name the third Indian war besides the Modoc war and Nez Perce war.
   a.  John Day war        b.  Rogue River war        c.  Platte River war

4. Name of the first steamboat built on the Willamette River.
   a.  The Columbia       b.  The Eagle               c.  Lot Whitcomb

5. The nickname for Portland was?
   a.  Stumptown          b.  Willyville              c.  Hardytown

6. Name the lady who helped Oregon get the vote for women.
   a.  Tabitha Brown       b.  Abigail Duniway       c. Narcissa Whitman

7. Who started a school that finally was named Pacific University?
   a.  Narcissa Whitman  b. Tabitha Brown           c. Abigail Duniway

8. The new capitol of Oregon was?
   a.  Salem                b. Oregon City            c. Eugene

9. Name the president who signed Oregon to be the 33rd state.
   a.  Thomas Jefferson    b. James K. Polk           c. James Buchanan

10. The Oregon Steam Navigation Co. was started by?
    a. Captain John Smith   b. Captain John Ainsworth        c. Captain Kid

### Matching

11._____  Government branch with judges.          A.  Feb. 14, 1859
12._____  Government branch with a governor.       B.  White Bird Canyon
13._____  Government branch with senators.         C.  Executive
14._____  Meaning of name for Chief Joseph.        D.  Col. Nelson Miles
15._____  Date of Oregon statehood.                E.  Legislative
16._____  Chief Joseph gave his rifle to?          F.  30
17._____  The two railroad men who fought each other.    G.  Grandmother's Land
18._____  The Nez Perce headed for?               H. Thunder Rolling  in the mountains
19._____  Number of days the Nez Perce had to leave their land?    I.   Judicial
20._____  The army attacked the Nez Perce at?      J.  Hill & Harriman

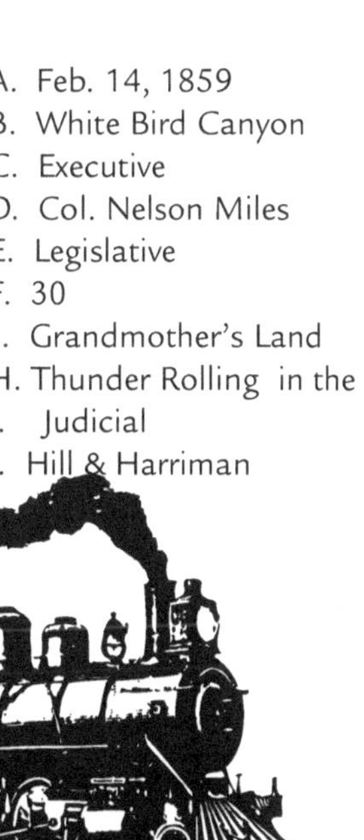

**Unit VI      Final Test      4 Points each**

## Fill in the blank:

1. Smoke from the  a.___________________  ____________could be seen all the way to  b. ___________________.
2. The fire was started by ______________________.
3. At Fort Rock Cave ________________________________ were found.
4. The word conifer comes from the word?________________
5. Portland is _______________ miles inland from the Pacific Ocean.
6. Number 3 dry-dock is located on ____________  _______________________.
7. Name one type of dairy cow. ______________________.
8. In World War I, ________________________ were made of spruce wood.
9. The Myrtle tree leaves smell like ______________________________.
10. The Goodyear Aerospace company made the ____________ - ________________________.

## Matching:

11. ______The smell of the Juniper berry.          A. mistletoe
12. ______Sheep production ranks.                  B. Salem
13. ______Name of the big 1933 fire.               C. second
14. ______The fire was caused by man's.            D. David Douglas
15. ______Grows in the tops of white oak trees.    E. carelessness
16. ______We can find a lot of fossils there.      F. 9000 yrs.
17. ______The Doug fir was named after?         G. pungent smell
18. ______A part of the laurel family.             H. John Day Fossil beds
19. ______How old were the sandals?                I.  Myrtlewood
20. ______Fruits and vegetables are frozen here.   J. Tillamook Burn

## Multipule Choice:

21. The man who found the sandals.
   A. Dr. L.S.Cressman   B. Dr. Marcus Whitman          C. Dr. John McLoughlin

22. Better storage and freezing methods were for?
   A. rabbits & quail       B. eggs & meat          C. wheat & lily bulbs

23. Sitka spruce trees can grow as tall as?
   A. 50 feet                B. 100 feet             C. 180  feet

24. The two kinds of trees we studied.
   A. fir and pine          B. broadleaf and needleaf          C. evergreen & deciduous.

## UNIT VII      FINAL TEST  4 points each

### Fill in the blank:

1.  The state capitol is located in __________________________________.
2.  The date Oregon became a state ________________________________.
3.  What are our state colors? __________________________________.
4.  Our state beverage is __________________________________.
5.  Oregon's state fish is the ______________ ______________.
6.  What is our state flower? __________________________________.
7.  The state bird of Oregon is? ______________ ______________.
8.  What is the state gemstone? ______________ ______________.
9.  The state rock is the ______________ ______________.
10. Name the state song. ____________ ________ ______________.

### Matching:

11. _____ Elevation of Mount Hood.          A. 36
12. _____ Major mountain range.             B. Square dance
13. _____ State insect.                     C. The Union
14. _____ Old state motto.                  D. 11,240 feet
15. _____ The state nut.                     E. "She Flies With Her Own Wings"
16. _____ Number of counties.               F. Oregon Swallowtail
17. _____ State seashell.                    G. Hazelnut
18. _____ New state motto.                   H. 1859
19. _____Date of statehood.                 I.  Cascade Range
20. _____State dance.                        J.  Oregon Hairy Triton

### Multipule choice:

21. The date of the first Provisional government was?
    a. 1843            b. 1859            c. 1805

22. The deepest lake in Oregon is.
    a. Klamath Lake        b. Crater Lake     c. Blue Lake

23. Oregon's state tree is the?
    a. maple            b. white oak        c.  Douglas fir

24. The major dams on the Columbia River are the Bonneville, Owhyee, John Day, McNary and?
    a. Bridger            b. The Dalles     c.  Pendleton

25.  The state animal is the?
    a. cougar            b. beaver            c. otter

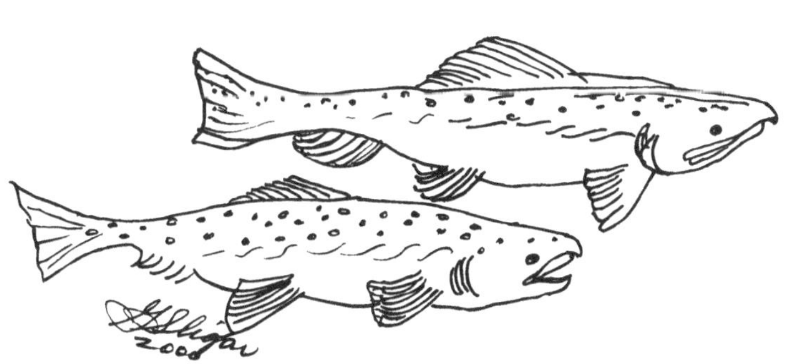

# UNIT VIII    FINAL TEST

## Two points each:        On a separate piece of paper:

1. List 18 of the 36 counties of Oregon.
2. List 18 of the 36 county seats.
3. Name one place to visit in each of the 18 counties you have just named.
4. Name the five major rivers in the state of Oregon.
5. Name the five major mountain ranges.

## Ten points each for a total of forty points:

Select four items from the "Facts of Oregon" found in Unit VII and write a 150-word report on each of the four.

## 50 points

Write a 250-word report on the county in which you live. Describe what makes your hometown and the county such a great place.

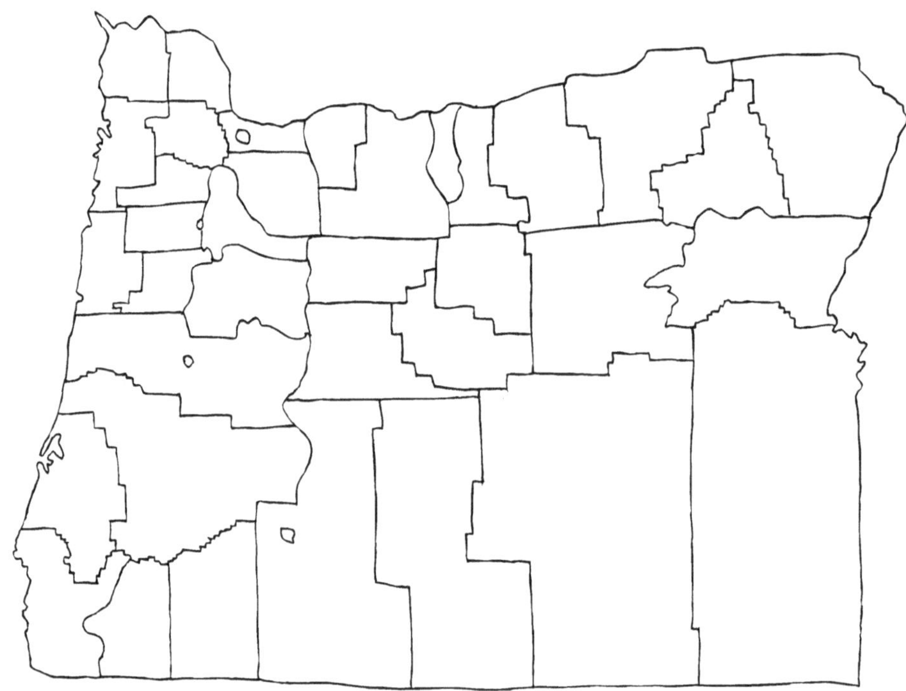

www.ingramcontent.com/pod-product-compliance
Lightning Source LLC
Chambersburg PA
CBHW040156110726
48005CB00018B/2790